501 WAYS
To Say

"I Love You"

(Or Words To That Effect)

By Babe Hart

501 WAYS
TO SAY
"I Love You"
(Or Words To That Effect)

© Copyright 1989 Babe Hart
Box 229, Woodland Hills, CA 91365

Manufactured in the United States of America

ISBN 0-9615829-5-2

Library of Congress
Catalog Card No. 88-92342

Published by:
        Baja Books, P.O. Box 4151
        Santa Barbara, CA 93140

Dedicated to Lovers
... Whoever You Are

With thanks to friends and
relatives for their kind
contribution. Lovers All.

Edited by T.L. Hart and
Dorothea M. Heitz

501 WAYS

To Say

"I Love You"

(OR WORDS TO THAT EFFECT)

By Babe Hart

CONTENTS

Introduction 1

The Basics 3

Romantic ... Pick-A-Phrase 5

Body Language 17

Adjectives 21

Nouns 29

Song Titles and Phrases 33

Foreign Language "I Love You's" 39

Sample Love Letters 42

Conclusion 88

About The Author 89

501 WAYS
TO SAY
"I Love You"
(OR WORDS TO THAT EFFECT)

Having trouble saying those three little words? Are you looking for the right phrase to express your feelings to your lover (mate?), lover-to-be or that special friend?

There are many ways to tell a person you care without having to use those most difficult-to-say words, "I Love You," and this book is designed to give you choices.

Find the words or phrases in the text which you feel are appropriate to your situation, whether humorous or serious, romantic or down-to-earth. Make it easy on yourself. Don't sweat it! Use this book as a go-by and have fun doing it.

Song titles are full of love feelings. We have included some of those fine words and phrases, plus examples of their use in letters.

Sometimes it is easier and more romantic to say " I Love You" in a foreign language, so we have included a section for that purpose plus numerous samples of love letters.

Easiest of all ... Give your lover a copy of the book with the phrases underlined or listed by number which say what you want to express in the love department ... and if all else fails, there is always No. 501.

Good luck! Bonne Chance! ¡Buena Suerte!

Go For it!

THE BASICS

Getting down to brass tacks:

1.   Baby, I need you.

2.   Your body is an invitation to love.

3.   Let's leave the world behind.

4.   Wanna make it with me?

5.   I long to caress every bit of you.

6.   I want you more than I can say.

7.   I go for the passionate embrace.

8.   I am in ecstasy when I am with you.

9.   You are flame and fire, and I am the match.

10.   I ache to touch you all over.

11.   I crave your kisses.

THE BASICS, Cont'd.

12.   Our vibes are harmonious.

13.   I hanker after you.

14.   Your kisses leave me breathless.

15.   I am in paradise when you are near.

16.   Baby, I'm bad.

17.   Baby, You're hot.

18.   Touch me and I'll melt.

19.   You're cool and that's bad.

20.   *Are you accessible?

21.   *Are you discreet?

22.   *I'm safe. Are you safe?

23.   *Trust me.

24.   *Don't worry, I'll respect you in the morning.

*(Sometimes the frank approach is the best prelude to love)

ROMANTIC

Pick - a - Phrase . . .

25.   I didn't live until I met you.

26.   Life has no meaning without you.

27.   You know how much I care about you.

28.   I want to spend the rest of my life making love to you.

29.   I just want to please you.

30.   You are everything to me.

31.   You are the sun, the moon and the stars.

32.   You are the light of my life.

33.   I live only for you.

34. I adore you.

35. Without you I am nothing.

36. You are wonderful.

37. You know you are my sweetheart.

38. I will do anything in the world for you.

39. You are what dreams are made of.

40. You are my dreams come alive.

41. You have my head spinning.

42. I am head over heels in love with you.

43. You are all I've wished for.

44. You are adorable.

45. Just to look at you gives me pleasure.

46. You thrill me.

47.   I feel amorous when I think of you.

48.   I long to hold you in my arms.

49.   I desire you more than I can say.

50.   You are my darling.

51.   You are very dear to me.

52.   My affection for you knows no bounds

53.   You have captured my heart.

54.   You have me bewitched.

55.   You are (my beloved).

56.   You are precious to me.

57.   I am exceptionally fond of you.

58.   I will be devoted to you forever.

59.   I swear my lifelong devotion to you.

ROMANTIC, Cont'd.

60. My heart is yours.

61. My arms long to caress you.

62. I have my heart set on you.

63. You fire my imagination.

64. I have taken a fancy to you.

65. Please let me love you.

66. You take my breath away.

67. I am spellbound.

68. I am speechless around you.

69. You are very desirable.

70. My feeling for you is indescribable.

71. You have brought me to life again.

72. Together we make a statement.

73. You are my one and only.

74. Where have you been all my life?

75. You are my lovelight.

76. I pine for you.

77. I am lonely without you.

78. My dreams of you sizzle.

79. I'm having a heat wave over you.

80. Let's get physical.

81. I'm entertaining wonderful thoughts of you.

82. You appeal to my finer senses.

83. I surrender, dear.

84. To dream of you is bliss.

85. I treasure you.

86. I promise you my undying love.

87. You are forever a part of me.

88. Share my life.

89. You are an inspiration.

90. You are my fountain of happiness.

91. With you my life will be complete.

92. Let us build a house of love.

93. My love for you is beyond passion.

94. Let's be intimate.

95. You make me shiver with anticipation.

96. My soul is dedicated to you.

97. Let's make it permanent.

98. Let's have a tie that binds.

99. I press you to my heart.

100. You are the best thing that ever happened to me.

101. I'd like to make permanent arrangements with you.

102. You want commitment? I'm yours.

103. You mean so much to me.

104. You are the last word.

105. You are my fantasy come true.

106. You are my ideal.

107. I'm stuck on you.

108. I'm sweet on you.

109. You have bowled me over.

110. You are the finest person I've ever known.

111. You are the one love of my life.

ROMANTIC, Cont'd.

112. Without you my life is empty.

113. With you my life takes on new meaning.

114. You bring joy to my world.

115. I want to give you everything.

116. You are heaven to me.

117. You are my desire.

118. I am ecstatic over you.

119. The day we met was a red-letter day.

120. You have my avid attention.

121. You are spectacular.

122. You are unbelievably attractive.

123. You are the ultimate.

124. You are like wine to my senses.

125. You have charmed me completely.

126. I kiss your fingertips.

127. I burn from the memory of your touch.

128. You are my woman.

129. You are my man.

130. My lips want to brush your throat.

131. You are my little dove.

132. You are my heartthrob.

133. You have the fragrance of a rose.

134. I have a fever burning for you.

135. You are my goddess of joy.

136. Your every movement is erotic.

137. I worship your naked body.

138. You breathe fire into me.

139. You are so sensuous.

140. I fly when I am with you.

141. Your lips are like wine.

142. I quiver with desire for you.

143. My thoughts of you make me blush.

144. You are the greatest.

145. Let's take time to love.

146. My heart beats for you.

147. You're always on my mind.

148. I want to love all of you.

149. I'll never leave you, my love.

150. You can depend on me.

ROMANTIC, Cont'd.

151. You are the cat's pajamas.

152. You're the best.

153. I tremble at your touch.

154. You are a delight to be with.

155. You're the cream in my coffee.

156. You're the crême de la crême.

157. You're the most.

158. You are one in a million.

159. You're the tops.

160. You're a winner.

161. You are A-number-one in my book.

162. I'm wild about you.

163. You are my hero.

ROMANTIC, Cont'd.

164. You are my heroine.

165. You appeal to me deeply.

166. Everything about you is real.

167. You are divine.

168. You are everything to me.

169. You are sublime.

170. My feelings for you run deep.

171. Be sure of my love.

172. I've never felt like this before.

173. Let me stay in your corner of the world forever.

BODY LANGUAGE

MAN TO WOMAN . . .

For use on women with a firm sense of the ridiculous.
These phrases are not guaranteed to work for you. But
who knows?

174. You have pretty feet..big, but pretty.

175. I like the way you smell. Your perfume is nice too.

176. You're smarter than you look, but then you'd have

    to be.

177. Your eyes are like limpid pools.

    (Whatever that means.)

178. Your cheeks have the lovely bloom of a sunburn.

179. Nobody looks like you do.

180. I love how your nose wrinkles when you are disgusted.

181. You have a dainty waist . . . I can almost get my arms around it.

182. Your hips are full of promise.

183. You are a heavenly handful.

184. Your neck is as long as a swan's . . . but graceful.

185. Your hands are as youthful as your mother's.

186. I'd like to kiss your pouty lips.

187. The back of your knee is my favorite spot.

188. I adore you, wrinkles and all.

189. No, you're not fat, just pleasingly plump.

BODY LANGUAGE, Cont'd.

WOMAN TO MAN . . .

Even if he gets turned off, he'll be glad you noticed him and he'll believe you.

190. You have such broad shoulders.

191. I admire heavy thighs.

192. I am wild to run my fingers through your hair.

193. Bald men appeal to me.

194. Your brows are awfully thick, but expressive.

195. Your biceps are grandiose.

196. Your ears wiggle when you leer at me.

197. Your mind interests me immensely.

198. Your pot belly is just right for patting.

199. I love hairy chests.

BODY LANGUAGE, Cont'd.

200. I adore your macho manner.

201. Your walk spells charisma.

202. Your mouth is a magnet.

203. Your body entices me.

204. When you flex, I think sex.

205. Your eyes undress me, and I am getting cold.

206. Ooh! You're so strong!

207. I like bowlegged men.

208. You have that rugged look I love.

VOCABULARY

Pick a word or words from this list of descriptive adjectives and nouns to include in your notes to friends, mates or lovers. Whatever is appropriate to the occasion.

ADJECTIVES:

EX: *You are so ...*

209.	adorable
210.	affectionate
211.	agreeable
212.	alert
213.	alive
214.	alluring
215.	ambrosial
216.	amiable
217.	amorous
218.	ardent
219.	arousing
220.	attractive
221.	bawdy
222.	beautiful
223.	breathtaking
224.	bright
225.	broadminded

ADJECTIVES, Cont'd.

226.	candid
227.	capricious
228.	captivating
229.	caring
230.	charming
231.	comely
232.	comforting
233.	considerate
234.	constant
235.	courteous
236.	dainty
237.	dandy
238.	dapper
239.	dazzling
240.	delicate
241.	delicious
242.	delightful
243.	demonstrative
244.	demure
245.	dependable
246.	desirable
247.	devoted
248.	divine
249.	dulcet
250.	elegant
251.	enchanting
252.	endearing
253.	endowed

ADJECTIVES, Cont'd.

254.	engaging
255.	enthusiastic
256.	enticing
257.	entrancing
258.	erotic
259.	exciting
260.	exotic
261.	exuberant
262.	fair
263.	faithful
264.	fantastic
265.	fascinating
266.	feminine
267.	fiery
268.	gallant
269.	generous
270.	gentle
271.	glorious
272.	glossy
273.	glowing
274.	goodlooking
275.	gorgeous
276.	graceful
277.	handsome
278.	heavenly
279.	heart-stirring
280.	honest

281.	honorable
282.	hot
283.	human
284.	ideal
285.	impetuous
286.	individualistic
287.	inimitable
288.	intellectual
289.	intelligent
290.	intoxicating
291.	jaunty
292.	keen
293.	lascivious
294.	liberal
295.	lovely
296.	loving
297.	loyal
298.	luscious
299.	macho
300.	maddening
301.	magnanimous
302.	magnificent
303.	manly
304.	modest

305.	natural
306.	observant
307.	out-of-sight
308.	out-of-this-world
309.	passionate
310.	perceptive
311.	pleasing
312.	pleasurable
313.	pretty
314.	princely
315.	provocative
316.	quixotic
317.	radiant
318.	ravishing
319.	red-hot
320.	refreshing
321.	resplendent
322.	responsive
323.	roguish
324.	romantic
325.	saintly
326.	seductive
327.	seemly
328.	sensational
329.	sensible

330.	sensitive
331.	sensuous
332.	sexy
333.	shapely
334.	shameless
335.	sleek
336.	sociable
337.	special
338.	splendid
339.	stupendous
340.	sublime
341.	superb
342.	sweet
343.	talented
344.	tantalizing
345.	tempting
346.	thrilling
347.	thoughtful
348.	true
349.	trusting
350.	understanding
351.	unmatched
352.	unparalleled
353.	upbeat
354.	upright
355.	unselfish

ADJECTIVES, Cont'd.

356.	virtuous
357.	voluptuous
358.	wanton
359.	warmhearted
360.	willing
361.	winsome
362.	wonderful
363.	youthful
364.	yummy

ADVERBS:

Need a few adverbs besides "so" to modify the above

adjectives? Try these:

You are..

Ex:	absolutely	(yummy)
	amazingly	(wanton)
	astonishingly	(youthful) etc.

especially
exceedingly
exceptionally
extraordinarily

ADVERBS, Cont'd.

graciously
gratifyingly
marvelously
passionately
sensuously
sexily
simply
temptingly
undeniably
unusually
wonderfully

NOUNS:

Use these nouns in such fashion as . . .
I am well aware of your *charm*, or
I am really delighted by your *generosity*, or
I am stunned by your *beauty*, or
I appreciate your *honesty*.

365.	affection
366.	allure
367.	amiability
368.	attentiveness
369.	beauty
370.	bravery
371.	charm
372.	comeliness
373.	consideration
374.	courtesy
375.	daring
376.	devotion
377.	elegance
378.	enthusiasm
379.	exuberance

380.	fairness
381.	fidelity
382.	friendship
383.	gallantry
384.	generosity
385.	good looks
386.	grace
387.	honesty
388.	humanity
389.	liveliness
390.	loyalty
391.	machismo
392.	magnetism
393.	magnificence
394.	manliness
395.	passion
396.	perception
397.	perfection
398.	polish
399.	radiance
400.	refinement
401.	sensitivity
402.	sexiness
403.	seductiveness

NOUNS, Cont'd.

404.	spirit
405.	splendor
406.	style
407.	talent
408.	tenderness
409.	thoughtfulness
410.	virility
411.	winsomeness
412.	wit
413.	zest
414.	zip

WITH ALL MY LOVE

I'll write you ev' ry day with all my love . . .
all my love . . . .   all my love . . . .
And with each word I'll send you
all my love . . . .   all my love . . .

You are so far a-way . . .
And on the lone - ly nights there'll come
to me . . . the ten-der thought of you . . .
to touch my mem - o - ry.

I'd like to keep your face be-fore my eyes . . .
Hear your voice, and re - a - lize
your arms are reaching out to cra - dle me,
then ev' - ry hour with you will I re - call
WITH ALL MY LOVE!

© Babe Hart

SONG TITLES

and

Phrases Which May Say It For You

415. You Do Something To Me.

416. I Get A Kick Out Of You.

417. I Am Yours Body And Soul.

418. I Only Have Eyes For You.

419. The Very Thought Of You (And I forget to do..the very things that everyone ought to do.)

420. You Go To My Head.

421. You Belong To Me.

422. No Other Love Can Warm My Heart.

423. I Am Yours Forever.

SONG TITLES and PHRASES, Cont'd.

424. Because Of You There's A Song In My Heart.

425. I Can Smile Because Of You.

426. I'm In Love With You, Honey.

427. Why Not Take All Of Me?

428. Don't Blame Me For Falling In Love With You.

429. I Don't Want To Set The World On Fire..I Just

Want To Start A Flame In Your Heart.

430. Let's Fall In Love.

431. Lover, Come Back To Me.

432. My Love Is Forever True.

433. There Was No One Till You.

434. I'm In Heaven When I See You Smile.

435. You'll Never Know Just How Much I Care.

SONG TITLES and PHRASES, Cont'd.

436. You Light Up My Life.

437. I Want To Hold Your Hand.

438. We Can Work It Out.

439. You Really Got A Hold On Me.

440. I've Got A Feeling I'm Falling.

441. Everything Your Heart Desires.

442. You Make My Dreams.

443. Never Gonna Give You Up.

444. Just Give Me One More Chance.

445. You Have Stolen My Heart.

446. I'll Be Your Baby Tonight.

447. Had A Dream About You, Baby.

448. Can't Help Falling In Love.

449. I Can't Stop Loving You.

450. Love Walked Right In.

451. I Found Someone.

452. You Are The Sunshine Of My Life.

453. What Are You Doing The Rest Of My Life?

454. You Are The Man I Love.

455. My Sweet Embraceable You.

456. It Had To Be You.

457. If I Could Be With You One Hour Tonight.

458. You Do Something To Me.

459. Yours Is My Heart Alone.

460. I Took One Look At You And Then My Heart
     Stood Still.

SONG TITLES and PHRASES, Cont'd.

461. You Are My Own True Love.

462. You Were Meant For Me.

463. All I Want Is Your Love.

464. Dream Lover.

465. My Heart Beats For You.

466. This Was Meant To Be.

467. I Am Under Your Spell.

468. I'll Be There For You.

469. I'm In The Mood For Love.

470. Let Me Call You Sweetheart.

471. I Idolize You.

472. You'd Be So Nice To Come Home To.

473. You'd Be So Easy To Love.

SONG TITLES and PHRASES, Cont'd.

474.   What A Feeling Is This!

475.   Oh, Give Me Something To Remember You By.

476.   Love Will Find A Way.

477.   Together Forever.

(Kudos to the composers whose

dreams become the songs).

OTHER LANGUAGES

. . . And sometimes it is easier to say "*I Love You*" in another language . . . Where a language, Chinese or Russian, for example, is usually written in characters or other forms such as Cyrillic, we will show the sound of the phrase as nearly as possible in parentheses.

478. Arabic . . . Ona Ohibic.
(<u>ah</u>-nah o-hee-bik)

479. Chinese . . . War i lee.
(wahr *ee* lee)

480. Danish . . . Jeg elsker dig.
(<u>yah</u>-ee <u>ehl</u>-skuh <u>dah</u>-ee)

481. Dutch . . . Ik houd van jou.
(ick howt von yow)

482. Finnish . . . Eakastan sinua.
(<u>eh</u>-ah-kah-stahn <u>si</u>-noo-ah)

483. French . . . Je t'aime (or) Je vous aime.
(zhuh tehm)   (zhuh voo-zehm)

OTHER LANGUAGES, Cont'd.

484. German . . .   Ich liebe dich.
                      (ickh lee-beh dikh)

485. Greek . . .   Saghapo.
                      (sahg-hah-poh)

486. Hawaiian . . .   Aloha wau ia oe.
                      (ah-loh-hah vah-oo ya oh-eh)

487. Hebrew . . .   (Ani ohev otakh)

488. Hindi . . .   (Mai tum-seh p'yahr kahr-teh hoo)
                      Man to Woman

                      (Mai tum-seh p'yahr kahr-tah hoo)
                      Woman to Man

489. Italian . . .   Ti voglio bene.
                      (tee voh-l'yoh beh-neh) or
                      Ti amo.
                      (tee ah-moh)

490. Irish (Gaelic) . . . (Mo graw too)

491. Japanese . . .   Ai shite masu.
                      (ah-ee shee-teh mah-soo)

492. Korean . . .   Na nun dang sin nul
                      sarang hap ni da.

493. Polish . . .   Kocham ciebie.
                        (<u>kohk</u>-ham chee-<u>yeh</u>-bee-<u>yeh</u>)

494. Portuguese . . .   Eu te amo.
                        (<u>eh</u>-oo teh <u>ah</u>-moh)

495. Russian . . .   Ya l'yoobloo vahs.
                        (yah lee-<u>oo</u>-bloo vahss)

496. (Serbo)
     Croatian . . .   Ja te lyubim.
                        (<u>yah</u> teh l'yoo-beem)

497. Spanish . . .   Yo te quiero.
                        (yoh teh k'<u>yeh</u>-roh)

498. Swedish . . .   Jag älskar dig.
                        (<u>yah</u>-ee <u>ehl</u>-skar deeg)

499. Tahitian . . .   Here vau ia oe.
                        (<u>heh</u>-reh <u>vah</u>-oo ee-<u>ah</u> oh-<u>eh</u>)

500. Vietnamese . . .   Anh Yêu Êm.
                        Man to Woman

     . . .   Êm Yêu anh.
                        Woman to Man

501.   . . . See Page 88 . . .

Writing a Love Letter:

Using the following as a go-by, pick phrases from the preceding pages which please you and which you feel will also please the one you love.

Example:

#	55	My Beloved.
#	332	You are undeniably sexy.
#	8	I am in ecstasy when I am with you.
# 228 & 344		You are captivating and tantalizing.
#	420	You go to my head.
#	5	I long to caress every bit of you.
#	418	I only have eyes for you.
#	65	Please let me love you.
#	497	Yo te quiero.

Put them all together in your letter:

My Beloved,

You are undeniably sexy. I am in ecstasy when I am with you. You are captivating and tantalizing. You go to my head and I long to caress every bit of you. Since I only have eyes for you, please let me love you.

Yo te quiero,

LOVE LETTERS, Cont'd.

These sample *"love letters"* straight from the heart may give you a head start. Check through your adjectives, nouns, song titles and foreign phrases and/or pick-a-phrase from the *Romantic* heading or from *Body Language* or from *Basic Phrases* to form a note that will say what you want it to say.

Example:

Dear Heart,

My affection for you knows no bounds. I want you more than I can say. I am speechless around you. You are so desirable that you have me bewitched.

Bothered and bewildered,

Dearest,

You do something to me. I can smile because of you, for you are the one I love. You are excruciatingly honest and yours is my heart alone. Lover, come back to me.

Je t'aime,

Darling,

    You are so natural and refreshing and feminine. You have brought me to life again. You are spirited and responsive. Let's fall in love.

              Ich liebe dich,

My Own,

    I don't want to set the world on fire, I just want to start a flame in your heart.

    If I could be with you one hour tonight, there would be no other love.

    I am yours body and soul.

                   Forever,

Dear Friend,

You mean so much to me. You are a very special person in my life . . . always loyal and loving. I do appreciate you.

Fondly,

Dear . . .

I have missed you so much. I have wanted to call you and apologize . . . to let you know that I care. I find you especially endearing. Please forgive me.

Affectionately,

Dear Lover,

What a feeling is this! You are the sunshine of my life. You make my dreams and I can't help falling in love with you.

I am under your spell,

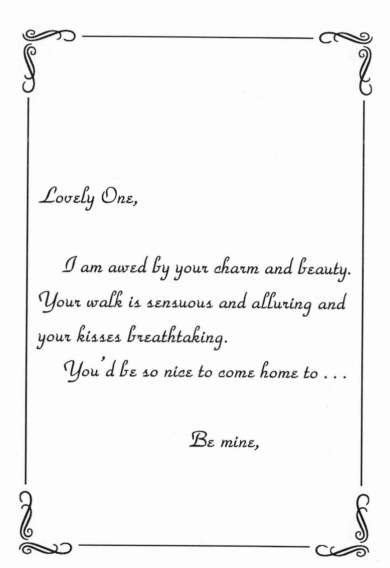

Lovely One,

I am awed by your charm and beauty.
Your walk is sensuous and alluring and
your kisses breathtaking.
You'd be so nice to come home to . . .

Be mine,

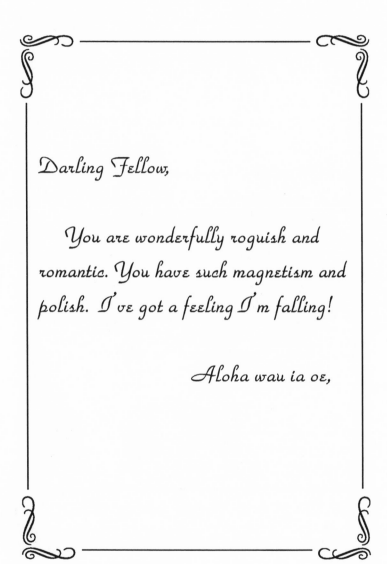

Darling Fellow,

You are wonderfully roguish and romantic. You have such magnetism and polish. I've got a feeling I'm falling!

Aloha wau ia oe,

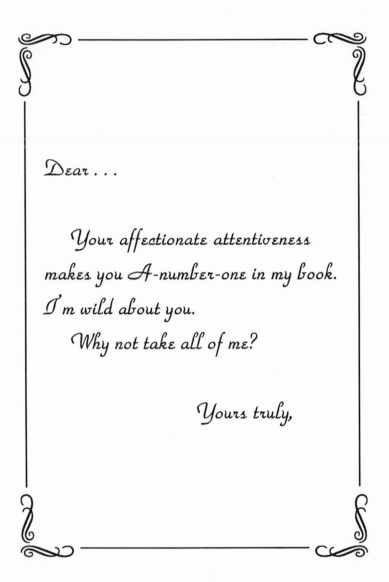

Dear . . .

Your affectionate attentiveness makes you A-number-one in my book. I'm wild about you.
Why not take all of me?

Yours truly,

Dream Lover,

You are exceptionally upright and warmhearted. Your princely manners are unmatched.

You are very dear to me.

Cordially,

LOVE LETTERS, Cont'd.

Sweetheart,

You are the ultimate —— like wine to my senses. You bring joy to my world. My heart is yours.

Love and kisses,

54

LOVE LETTERS, Cont'd.

Loved one,

I tremble at your touch. My thoughts of you make me blush. You're always on my mind. You are passionate and intensely provocative . . .

I hunger for you,

LOVE LETTERS, Cont'd.

Using phrases from "Body Language," you might have fun writing something like this (if appropriate).

MAN TO WOMAN . . .

Dear One,

You have a dainty waist . . . I can almost get my arms around it and I have tried, as you know . . . but I adore you, wrinkles and all.

No, you are not fat, just pleasingly plump. Anyway, you're smarter than you look. But then you'd have to be.

How about getting together?

Yours 'til the cows come home,

LOVE LETTERS, Cont'd.

WOMAN TO MAN . . .

Macho Man,

    Bald men appeal to me and when I spot your pot belly, I just have to pat it.
    I'd like to lean on your broad shoulders and run my fingers through your hair, but then you don't have any to speak of, do you? Anyway, I am

    Yours in anticipation,

LOVE LETTERS, Cont'd.

And if it's the real thing . . .

My love,

Though we have been apart, I hope that distance will not dim the power of the feelings we have for each other.

We must hold to our beliefs of love and expect only the best. Let us try fervently to be together in time and though our love be tested in many ways, we shall reaffirm it in our letters as vividly as if we were together.

This I do, for I think of you constantly and long for the day when we can put our arms around each other and be close forever more.

More in love than ever,

LOVE LETTERS, Cont'd.

And there's loving friendship . . .

Dear Friend,

I bless the day you were born. You have shown me such kindness. Your thoughtful words and deeds have helped me get through many a trying hour.

Just knowing you are there for me if I need you has meant a lot to me.

Even though I may not show my deep appreciation as often as I should, I do hope that this note will express to you my warmest regards.

You are a very important person in my life and you have my heartfelt gratitude for being my friend.

Most sincerely,

LOVE LETTERS, Cont'd.

Now go all out on your own and let your imagination soar.

Perhaps these love letters will inspire you:

Dear . . .

If love is just a game, I still want to play it as long as you do.
We could both be winners.

Let's try it,

LOVE LETTERS, Cont'd.

Darling,

    I treasure our moments together even more when we are apart.

    There is a burning in my soul and a yearning in my heart to be with you night and day.

    You are ever in my thoughts.

                Affectionately,

Dear . . .

Let me be with you to see what you see, feel what you feel, be a part of you. I don't want to ever let you go.

Stay with me,

Darling,

I am tempted by you. My daydreams are full of wild expectations. I picture us in strange exotic places filling our nights with love things, forgetting time and ignoring people.

Do you dream the same dream?

As ever,

63

Dear . . .

You surprise me. Each time we are together you surprise me. And fill my heart with delight.

and love,

Dear . . .

    Are you teasing me with your very shameless flirting? Do you tease others in the same way? Or am I the only one? I'd like to be . . . . and . . . . then I wouldn't mind.

                      Wonderingly,

Dearest,

You know that I long to feel your heartbeat, hold you so close that we almost stop breathing and then smother you with kisses.

You can lay your head upon my pillow anytime.

Ever yours,

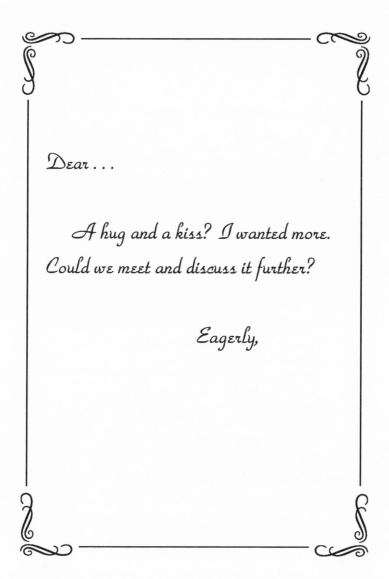

Dear . . .

A hug and a kiss? I wanted more.
Could we meet and discuss it further?

Eagerly,

LOVE LETTERS, Cont'd.

Dear . . .

The sweet memory of your presence envelops my room with the essence of love.

This space so recently filled with enchantment now leaves me dreaming of your return.

Will that be soon? I want you near me always.

Lovingly,

Dear . . .

Have you cast a spell upon me? I cannot sleep, cannot eat.

I think of our loving adventure and wonder if it is just spring fever . . . or will it last through summer, fall and winter?

It must, it must,

69

Dear . . .

I want to hold on to you. Lead you along the path to love —— share my deepest emotions with you and always be where you are. Will you allow me?

Yours,

70

Dear . . .

Can you read between the lines?
Please look closely and find there a
depth to my feeling for you that I cannot
always express openly.

But I am trying,

Dear,

There is suddenly a rainbow in my sky. It was not there before I met you.

My world is bright again with the desire for you filling my heart.

Love,

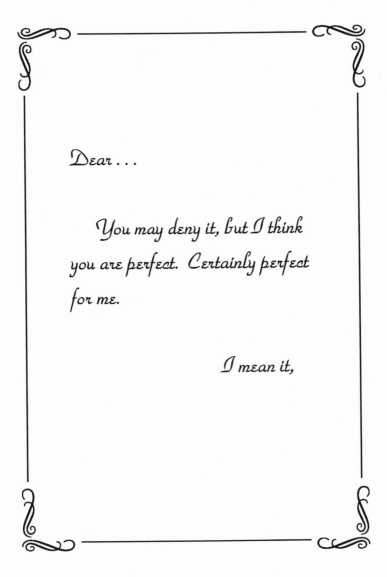

Dear . . .

You may deny it, but I think you are perfect. Certainly perfect for me.

I mean it,

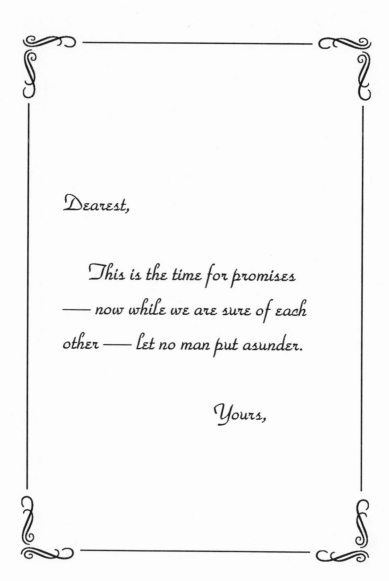

Dearest,

This is the time for promises — now while we are sure of each other — Let no man put asunder.

Yours,

LOVE LETTERS, Cont'd.

Dear . . .

    I felt bonded to you the moment we met. Do you think we were as one in a former life?

    We must have loved before. Will we love again?

        Yours,

Dearest,

You are an original. There is a magic about you that excites me and distracts me. I must see more of you.

Hoping,

My darling,

I find myself taking deep breaths and sighing over you.

Could we get together and celebrate my discovery? You?

Full of desire,

77

Dear . . .

Is it possible to love too much? If so, then that is my dilemma. I am lost without you.

Be with me again,

Dear . . .

You are a challenge! I want to peek beneath the mask.

I know there is a fiery passion hiding there.

Will you let me see it?

Longingly,

LOVE LETTERS, Cont'd.

Dear ...

Your tenderness shows me that you are an understanding person. That means a lot to me.

I hope we continue to see each other and let fate show us the way.

Fondly,

Dear . . .

Sometimes hidden feelings are suddenly fanned into a flame by a look, a word, a touch.

This is what happened to me when last we were together. I did not realize before how much you meant to me . . .

I do now,

LOVE LETTERS, Cont'd.

Adored one,

I am feeling gloriously alive with memories of our time together.

Loving, loving, loving,

Loving you,

Dear . . .

Dreams of you occupy my days
and my nights. You are in my head
and I can think of nothing else,
dreaming of your touch, your warmth.
Please come to me soon.

With love,

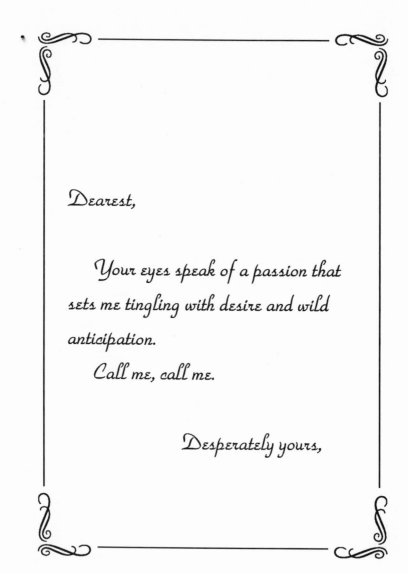

Dearest,

Your eyes speak of a passion that sets me tingling with desire and wild anticipation.

Call me, call me.

Desperately yours,

Dear . . .

There is an air of enchantment about you. I am both puzzled and entranced.

Why have I not realized before what an extraordinary person you are. Your face is carved in my mind.

I must see you again.

Please,

Dear one,

I am in my room. The moonlight is shining through the trees and making mysterious shadows play on the wall.

I cannot sleep because I want you here beside me.

I need you.

Hear me,

Dearest,

Shall we find an island to ourselves? Where we can lie in the sand, swing in the hammock, make love under the palm trees and pretend it is forever?

I'd like that,

And in Conclusion . . . . .

No. 501

P. S.

I

Love

You

Besides being the author of *"501 Ways To Say I Love You, (Or Words To That Effect),"* Babe Hart, a graduate of the University of Colorado, has authored the book entitled *"A Pocketful of Poems."* She is also the originator of "Speedy Language Phrase-books" for travelers and is a songwriter member of ASCAP.

Ciao!